# The Return
# of the Gobshite

Poetry that is inspirational,
motivational, feeds your soul and
makes you think with a smile.

## Mick Larkin

# THE AUTHOR

Welcome to book two of poems of wisdom and knowledge. Every poem was written in less than 10-15 minutes. As my Angels and Spirit Guides give me inspiration, the words just flow out of me onto the page. These books are my journey and my path to travel. As a psychic medium, I connect with my guides daily. The lessons and intuitive learning they have given me are now shared with you all, through this book.

As a podcaster with numerologist Grainne Tyndall, (Numbers4Success,- Gobshites on tour) we get to bring huge learning in a fun setting, like the poems. I know as you read these poems you will find yourself questioning your path here and they will give you food for thought, healing, inspiration, and wisdom. As we all evolve to the 5th dimension, I remember fondly my first platform with Moira Geary and the positive Recombobbers whom continue to support my writings. Thanks to all those who supported my first book, I never expected it to be such a success.

Thank you
Mick Larkin

**Podcast :**  Numbers4Success
          Gobshites on tour

**Instagram:**  ramblingsofagobshite

**Book available from :**  All books (Portlaoise)
          Wicklow holistic centre
          Stan and Tony's (Wicklow)
          Mick Quinn (Glendalough)
          Larkinmick@hotmail.com

# CONTENTS

# The book of life

When I see my reflection
The person I now see
Is not now the person
That I once used to be

Some say I am different
Others say I am strange
They just don't realise
It's important to change

As wisdom does come
More often with age
This book of our life
Is lived page by page

You are your own pen
Your mind is your page
You make the character
That performs on stage

You learn to be satisfied
You meet life with decision
You manifest your future
With a positive vision

But know the importance
Of peace and solitude
And of course the need
To have a love of gratitude

We never can know
What will be pending
It's only the higher power
That writes down the ending

*ML 2022*

---

Your mind is your pen, so make sure you write your own amazing story.

## My ego and me

I looked in the mirror
My ego it was there
You're not looking bad
But go brush your hair

I took in on board
Went for the brush
But then I decided
There is no real rush

But the feeling arose
I'm not at my best
It nagged at my brain
It was killing my zest

Why do you crave
To always be great
Sometimes its so nice
To just be in a state

If people won't listen
The interest isn't there
Tell them it's a secret
They will listen and stare

We all have an ego
Befriend it and smile
Acknowledge it's good
And wear it with style

But don't let it rule
The way that you act
That can be seen
As having no tact

*ML 2022*

---

Our egos can often be our down fall. If you work or live your life from a place of ego you are in trouble. Only your arrogance will shine.

# Heaven for an hour

I was asked one day
To visit heaven for an hour
It was a gift from above
To show me the real power

Along came an Angel
It said I'm your guide
There is no need to worry
I will be by your side

Time was non existent
My family were all there
They welcomed me in
Sat me down on a chair

We are all here together
No one did ever die
That is a human concept
It is such a terrible lie

Your purpose on this earth
Is to evolve and grow
Into the energy of love
Those seeds, you now sow

They all gave me hugs
We will always be here
As I left with my Angel
I no longer had fear

I returned to my body
My brain had no clue
But my soul it did know
That my visit was so true

*ML 2022*

---

What a wonderful place heaven, or whatever you want to call it, is.
A place of unconditional love.

## A thought or two

When you live your life
In that horrible fast lane
It just simply means
You die quicker in vain

Buy with your eyes
Don't buy with your ears
If you listen to others
Your decisions not clear

People on committees
They're a group of unwilling
Who don't want to be there
They are paddling and filling

Some people do state
You are your biggest fan
When asked why I do it
Sure it's because I can

When in times of stress
And you're in total despair
You can change the mood
By saying a little prayer

A boss tries to bully
A leader, they do inspire
A boss drags you down
A leader lights your fire

Wealth, happiness and love
Feel best when you share
Keeping it to yourself
Leaves you empty and bare

*ML 2022*

---

Several little nuggets of wisdom. Enjoy yourself, pray a little, inspire those around you, and share the wealth.

## Life's little steps

First you are born
You're this bundle of joy
In order to get comfort
All you did was cry

Then you start growing
The years they move fast
You eat, drink, and play
Sure life is a blast

As you get older
You learn there's rules
Your told to learn them
They are your life's tools

Your smile starts to fade
Your now in this race
To accomplish your goals
Life has increased its pace

Without even knowing
You have lost that child
Who played all the time
Whose dreams were wild

You were programmed
That life should be tough
Nothing should come easy
And at times it got rough

Although these programmes
Are embedded real deep
Once you delete and reset
You no longer will weep

For life is for living
Go back to that time
Playing made you happy
Without rules that define

*ML 2022*

---

We are born to have fun, but unfortunately the programming we undergo changes the whole way in which we act.

## Energy of life

Think of your energy
As being like cash
Would you waste it away
Or dump it like trash

Would you give your cash
To people you just meet
Then why give your energy
That just leads to defeat

Think of your energy
Like it's the Bank of you
And how you invest it
Will decide how you do

You need all your energy
To create tomorrow's dream
Without it your paddling
Against the flow of the stream

Your energy is important
It protects your field
It surrounds your body
It's your invisible shield

Saving up your energy
Now that is the trick
It's like building your wall
It's done brick by brick

You can conserve energy
Just change your attitude
But we have to get rid
Of the inept platitudes

*ML2022*

---

Your energy is your life force, stop wasting it on useless projects
and energy vampires.

## Resistance

Am I now in resistance
To what I once did
Am I in my safe box
With a very closed lid

Am I happily resistant
Am I happy on my own
Is your life being lived
Through your mobile phone

What now in my life
Needs to be lifted
There are things we can do
Once old energy is shifted

You are your hamster
You're on your own wheel
With the thoughts of change
Is it anxiety that you feel

If you dance to the beat
Of your own safe drum
Maybe now is the time
To get off your bum

Pretend you are eighty
Was being safe your thing
That's like being a guitar
But without any string

You went through life
No music did you make
If those are your memories
You need a good shake

*ML 2022*

---

Know your resistance to things, recognise it and deal with it, leave your legacy.

## Looking back

Well here I am now
Sure I'm eighty eight
All that's before me
Is heaven's big gate

I look back at my life
I wonder out loud
I learned from mistakes
Of that I am proud

I was kind and gentle
I done no one harm
My smile was infectious
And worked like a charm

I was a lovable rogue
A keeper of the faith
One lesson I learned
You are your best mate

I loved unconditionally
I gave one hundred percent
To those who knew me
I was such a nice gent

Friends I had so many
But none were so true
As those who could vibrate
And ground themselves too

Source it did call me
Sent me Angels galore
Spirit Guides to channel
Wisdom, teaching and more

My books there are many
Each one with a theme
Live life to the full
Don't be afraid to dream

*ML 2022*

---

Add thirty years to your age and look back at yourself from those shoes. Make sure you are happy with the vision you see.

## Leaving the World early

This was not my plan
Nothing can I change
But my soul is now free
I know that sounds strange

I know grief and sorrow
I did leave behind
But I could no longer be
In a life full of grind

To my family and friends
There is no reason why
My mind was irrational
My human logic I'd defy

To those I left behind
Forgive me I do ask
Trying to figure it out
Is such a heavy task

I showed no visible signs
Of weakness or of woe
My sudden departure
Was such a terrible blow

The fragility of the mind
Is invisible to most
It's not like you are sick
Or have a pallor of a ghost

I am now so very happy
I was not meant to stay
I have returned to source
For you now I pray

Now that my body is gone
I have but one request
To remember the good
When life was at its best

*ML 2022*

---

Suicide is an option some take, acknowledge it as a path to inner freedom for them.

## The art of forgiveness

Forgive us our trespasses
We all know the prayer
If you sit in forgiveness
It is such a great chair

When you are annoyed
Respect it's their view
It should never influence
How you think of you

If you now do forgive
You release all the crap
Your joy it won't hinder
Or happiness it won't sap

You don't have to say
I forgive you your action
Don't hold the bad energy
It should not be a distraction

Go up in your elevator
To your own fifth floor
Have that conversation
Then just walk out the door

It does not have to mean
You agree with the stance
We all have our own music
To which we do dance

When you decide to talk
Make all your words sweet
Just in case one fine day
Those words you may eat

*ML 2022*

---

Don't be afraid to forgive, it benefits you more than anyone else.

# A wake up call

I sit now and do wonder
Am I a little insane
As I miss how Covid
Put life in the slow lane

I am looking all around me
Our lives are now pushing
Us back on the clock
Where you're forever rushing

No more families do walk
The schedule they must fill
Pretending to be happy
But it's weariness they instil

We all know that feeling
Your now back in a trap
That wastes all your energy
Your living life in a flap

The Universe works away
Refocusing our intent
To calibrate a new life
New visions to invent

The Vortex is so full
Of all you have requested
Do meditate and align
It's time well invested

It's love and gratitude
We need to contemplate
Life is simply about caring
In order to feel great

*ML 2022*

---

As we return to normality, don't fall back into the rat race of life.
I did and the Universe kicked my butt back down to earth.

## Failure

What does failure mean
Is there no such thing
But everyone does learn
From the lessons it brings

If there was no failure
How could you feel
The joy of your success
For that feeling is real

Failure is the word given
To define an event
But if you gave it your best
It was time well spent

It's not whether you fail
But the action you took
It's patience and learning
It's just like writing a book

Be friends with your failure
It teaches us so much
But much more importantly
It keeps our reality in touch

Have you got the courage
To go attempt and fail
For it is only in failure
That the learning will unveil

Would not life be boring
If the risk was never there
It really is far better
Than sitting in your chair

*ML 2022*

---

Don't be afraid to fail, we all do daily and it's how we learn.

## Need

What really do I need
Is it a feeling of lack
If that is why you need
Cut yourself some slack

The need to do something
That's pressure and tough
It's angst and more stress
Can make life very rough

When I need something
It can be based on fear
It blocks all those thoughts
Common sense you can't hear

I need to do this
I need to do that
I need to be the best
It's the race of the rat

Instead of I need to
Say I choose this for me
But only when I'm ready
And my time is free

If we all lived now
From a place of no need
Happiness would bloom
Like the growth of a seed

To raise your vibration
Don't use the word need
Need comes from control
It's time to be freed

*ML 2021*

---

If we live needing stuff daily we will never be happy. Being needy is so sad.

## Ignorance is a choice

Where ignorance is bliss
Tis folly to be wise
If this is your space now
Unhappiness is your prize

Just because you hear it
Does it mean it's true
Ask the awkward question
See what comes to you

So how do I handle this
Will I sit out and wait
For more useless information
That weighs down my gait

All the negative rhetoric
Can only do one thing
The negativity you think
The Universe it will bring

Then we sit and wonder
My life just ain't great
Challenge all the garbage
It's so healthy to debate

I may refuse to listen
When my gut says it's wrong
It's easier to ignore it
You know you don't belong

The Universe for sure
Does go humble us all
From all the knowing
We often take a fall

Why climb in a window
When the door is open wide
Choose the door of knowledge
Ditch the 'know all' pride

*ML 2021*

---

We don't know everything, always be willing to learn.

## Happily ever NOW

If you want to be happy
Find your own definition
You live in a lifetime
That's so full of attrition

If I get my new job
Then I know I will be happy
Along comes the new job
But you're still feeling crappy

If I win some cash
I will be over the moon
But when it's all spent
Back comes the gloom

If I get a new house
A holiday from abroad
Surely I will be happy
That feelings a fraud

If I got my new car
That will make me smile
But that fades quickly
As I drive each mile

If you wait on happiness
To come to your door
You will wait a long time
Your life's now a chore

Be happy in the NOW
It's a decision you make
If you're waiting on happiness
That's your biggest mistake

*ML 2022*

---

Don't wait to be happy, be happy in the NOW. Every day is a blessing.

## Give praise

When you see beauty
In someone you know
Tell them all about it
Don't just let it go

Acknowledge the person
Who does something nice
It comes from their heart
Without having a price

That compliment you give
May lessen their blight
Increase their self love
Their confidence you ignite

At the end of the day
It's not what you do
It's the things that we don't
Hurt like a tight shoe

So make it your goal
To always praise and smile
The praise that you gave
Will last a long while

When a child grows up
It's attention they require
From the flame of praise
Can come a whole fire

Confidence like the wheel
Cannot be reinvented
But we can help inflate it
Make life more contented

*ML 2022*

---

Don't hesitate to compliment people, that small gesture can make someone's day.

## Drama, drama, drama

Drama, drama, drama,
What a place to be
Some people love it
Despite its toxicity

Did you hear the goss
Oh I heard it's true
Then they add a bit
That's how it all grew

They just can't wait
Whether truth or not
To spread the drama
And add to the plot

No thought is given
Everything is a fact
Of course it's delivered
Without an ounce of tact

The voice rings out
Omg did you hear that
Your inner wisdom goes
Omg what a prat

Don't pay any attention
To the useless chatter
Even if it's positive
It can deceive with flatter

Isn't it a beautiful place
When your drama free
Your bubble is zipped up
And the truth you do see

*ML 2021*

---

Avoid that third dimensional drama as much as possible. It's toxic.

## Carp Diem

The vibration of life
Is ours now to enjoy
If you are smiling
It means you can't cry

Seize the auld day
With two powerful hands
Don't just go settle
Sure it all will be grand

I own this very day
I decide what I will do
If your not feeling happy
You're now feeling blue

The opportunity of life
Is a precious gift
What can I achieve
That gives me a lift

Look in the mirror
Repeat just one thing
I can handle the rubbish
That life has to bring

I zip up my bubble
The fear, it won't win
No one can touch
The power from within

Finally you are amazing
When times are tough
You know you can take
The smooth with the rough

*ML 2022*

---

Seize the day, there is nothing you can't handle or there is nothing that won't pass.

# It's all in the knowing

I know, I know, I know
But it's not the case
Here are some examples
To cut through the chase

There are people around us
Who just do not know
They are just innocent
Please help them grow

There are people around us
Who know but don't know
Just go and wake them
To go join the show

There are people around us
Who are willing to know
Go teach them gladly
It's a gift you bestow

There are people around us
Who think that they know
Those people you avoid
They will halt your own flow

There are people around us
Who definitely do know
For their seeds of knowledge
Go plough a furrow

So who am I, where am I
Why am I now here
You KNOW you have this
It's your life to steer

*ML 2021*

---

Know yourself and let the Universe do the rest. Those who know will come to you.

## The fifth dimension

I sat and I meditated
I got into my lift
Up to the 5th dimension
My mindset did shift

Got out of the lift
I was on the 5th floor
I walked down a hall
Then I opened a door

The light was brilliant
The feeling was immense
I began to realise
I had come over the fence

There was no fear
No sound of ill will
You think I had swallowed
A happiness pill

Emotions were buzzing
My ego it was dead
All of my old past
Had been put to bed

Love it was abundant
I thought I would burst
The feeling of joyfulness
Was quenching my thirst

Negativity and influence
Were dragging me back
To the daily reality
Of the life that we hack

Now that I sampled
The beauty of the five
To that amazing place
For happiness I strive

*ML 2022*

---

The amazing fifth dimension is where we are all heading.
What an amazing place of unconditional love.

# Why did I not know

Why did I always criticise
Why did I always care
About silly stuff in life
I thought was not fair

Why did I not know
Life could be great
Instead of finding out
At heaven's big gate

Why did I suffer
The wrath of a fool
Allowing yourself
To be a foot stool

Why was I always
Thinking of the poor me
When I could of been
A powerful oak tree

Why in this World
Do we not understand
That everything we want
Is in our own hands

The answer is simple
We get signs galore
It is your own choice
To open the right door

If I had just known
What I think, I do, I be
It really was that simple
To live and be happy

*ML 2022*

---

No point in looking back at the past and asking why.
Look to the future and keep only positive thoughts.

# Character

Ah they are a great character
But what does it mean
That from their butt end
Shines the sun's light beam

Both the mental and moral
That is how we define
The character of someone
Whether it's bad or sublime

Some people judge character
By how people do dress
But it's ridiculously easy
To wear clothes that impress

Others will judge character
By the vehicle they may drive
Or the address where you live
Or the story you contrive

But a persons character
Is the choices they make
From the ingredients of life
We bake our own cake

The character of a person
Comes from life's mistakes
The error of one's judgement
Teaches what's true and fake

Your character is your morals
The decisions that you made
For a person with character
True goodness will cascade

*ML 2023*

---

Don't judge a character by the person they show you. Delve deeper to find the real person. Material trappings don't make good people.

## Archangel Michael

He is an angel
A powerful being
The likes of what
Has never been seen

You call upon him
In times of trouble
He will protect you
He is an amazing bubble

He wields a sword
Full of protection
Cutting the chords
That cause infection

His shield he uses
To protect us all
To negative energy
It's like a brick wall

If you need his help
You just have to ask
He will keep you safe
For him it's no task

The throat chakra
Is where he is found
Fifth dimensional wisdom
From there will astound

You can call upon him
To help you in need
His prayer of protection
Will help you indeed

*ML 2021*

---

When you need protection call in Archangel Michael, he is with you always.

# I'm not

I'm not going to listen
To people who moan
You close off that voice
Turn off that phone

I'm not going to think
Thoughts that are bad
I will only think things
That make me feel glad

I'm not going to worry
It's a waste of my time
I want the mindset
Where everything is fine

I'm not going to live
In this third dimension
Working your butt off
Just to get a pension

I'm not going to have
A pity party for two
That negative old energy
Bringing sadness to you

I'm not going to wonder
Why life can be tough
When in the reality
You are more than enough

I am going to smile
I am going to spread
The light of happiness
And gratitude instead

*ML 2022*

---

You control your own thoughts and decide what you think.

## You got this

You sit and wonder why
My thoughts are not in sync
Why am I thinking this way
Your head is on the blink

Nothing is now rational
Everything is in a spin
Even the most simple task
You don't want to begin

As you analyse the mood
You cannot find a reason
Why is your perception
And thoughts full of treason

Then a lightbulb moment
Thoughts are yours to rule
You are in charge of this
You are not a mindless fool

You take back the power
You live life day by day
And any time you do slip
It's still going to be okay

For without the darkness
You can't experience light
Everyone will struggle here
We all have done that fight

But once the fight is over
The lessons you did gain
Make you a better person
It was worth all of the pain

*ML 2022*

---

There is nothing you can't handle, remember that.

## Yea but

I want to go manifest
It's very easy to do
But along comes 'yea but'
Then it won't come true

I want to go change
The way that I think
But along comes 'yea but'
And you're back to the brink

I want to be happy
And smile even more
But along comes 'yea but'
Nothing good is in store

I hear that little voice
Go on be the best
But then comes 'yea but'
And I'm put to the test

I know I can do this
I have all the tools
But along comes 'yea but'
No you can't, you fool

How long will I listen
To this voice of doom
That just says 'yea but'
And adds to your gloom

Yea but, yea but, yea but
I'm putting you away
No longer will you rule
I'm controlling the play

*ML 2022*

---

We all know the 'yea but', time to ignore it and be the best you can.

## No more overwhelm

So your lying in the bed
Life is no longer here
The gates of heaven await
You have ended this career

Looking back I can see
Nothing really mattered
All the overwhelm I felt
Just left my body battered

I tried to please you all
I tried to be the best
But eventually I did realise
And done more things in jest

It took a while to learn
To treat life like a game
Life was meant to be
Enjoyed without shame

All you have are memories
Make sure they are great
Full of goodness and joy
As you roll up to the gate

But I never figured out
In the mirror as I look
Whether I was Peter Pan
Or was I Captain Hook

Now it's not important
I'm on the final mile
I ticked off all the things
That made my life worthwhile

*ML 2022*

---

Remember in the end it's only memories we have, make sure they are good ones.

# I am not gone

As I face the final hours
I dwell upon the past
I have no regrets here
My life was, oh so fast

Everyone around me
Is crying and distraught
I wish they would just focus
On the happiness I brought

The air it leaves my body
An Angel takes my hand
The waves of my life
Are crashing on the sand

I look up to the heavens
I see Peter at the gate
My Soul, it knows it's home
This trip is all our fate

Those I've left behind
Tears they now do shed
But it's only my body
That lies here on the bed

I guide them now daily
I protect them when in need
I'm the feather on the floor
The water for the seed

I'm just another Angel
I'm the beauty of a flower
My soul is soaring high
I am with the higher power

I am now an energy
You may feel despair
Yet I am with you
I am now everywhere

*ML 2022*

Do not fear death our bodies only die. Our souls live forever.

## Crystals of life

We all love our crystals
Their energetic power
It's cleansing for the body
It's an energy shower

Clear quartz a master healer
Rose quartz is for love
Pair both of them together
It's a gift from above

Ruby restores your vitality
Sapphire for wisdom and peace
Having these are vital
For negativity to cease

Jasper is supreme nurturer
To empower you in stress
Tigers eye for motivation
When you're in a mess

Obsidian the protective stone
Citrine brings joy and wonder
These protect your energy
From being torn asunder

Amethyst is for sincerity
Turquoise is for grounding
Both are really welcome
When your taking a pounding

Bloodstone is for your blood
Moonstone for inspiration
Which brings back success
And helps you with creation

Finally when you get crystals
You will have to cleanse away
Any attached negativity
Make them yours today

*ML 2022*

---

Our crystals are so important so cleanse them daily when in use.

## Abraham Hicks

So Abraham has told us
We are on the leading edge
Where knowledge and joy
Guide us on this ledge

Go now and do calibrate
With your inner being
So those who come to you
Are really worth seeing

I do love that Esther
Enjoys her basketball too
Abrahams use of the free throw
Made me smile right through

You know your expectation
Is both belief and desire
Make sure that your thoughts
Are fuelling that nice fire

When all of your thoughts
Are coupled with an emotion
If they are not positive
That's a very lethal potion

Our life here on this planet
Should be one of celebration
Don't surround yourself
With negative procrastination

Own how you now feel
Go raise your vibration
To the high flying disc
That's full of great elation

*ML 2022*

---

Abraham Hicks one of my favourite entities to listen to.

## The Knocking Spirit

I tossed and I turned
My sleep it was broke
I heard the knocking
Is this some kind of joke

I closed my ears off
But a breeze came in
It covered my body
Goose bumps to the chin

I reached for my phone
Three o'clock on the dot
It's the Angels calling
This is their time spot

I was awoke with a jolt
I was so fully awake
A whisper in my ear
You have notes to take

Into my sacred space
I sat down with my pen
The sage it was burning
I felt secure in my den

A voice it did speak
Spirit is his name
The energy was amazing
With wisdom he came

Then it was Dakota
My Indian spirit guide
He brings in the souls
From them you can't hide

With all my notes taken
I thank all who came in
Closed down my Chakras
And to bed with a grin

*ML 2022*

---

At night I get the knocking as the Angels love to make contact between 3am and 5am. So, if you are waking then pay attention to the messages.

## Recovering doer

You wake in the morning
Oh I have to do this
Your brain it takes off
Hoping nothing you miss

As you begin to awaken
Throw yourself out of bed
Your eyes barely open
But loads in your head

What will I go do first
Where is my to do list
Doing stuff for everybody
Hoping nothing missed

The value of your time
Is getting less and less
Yet all the while your life
To you feels like a mess

Then suddenly it happens
The penny it does drop
You spent time doing things
So your life was not a flop

But who really does care
It is just your inner fear
Hoping for that gratitude
Which oft was insincere

We no longer have to do
No lists now do we make
We decide when to eat
Make time for tea and cake

Finally I must admit
A doer is what I did
But now the things I do
For me, are at my bid

*ML2023*

---

Doing everything for everyone else is a problem for us all. Now it's time to put yourself first.

# Manipulators

Manipulators are people
Really not very nice
Every action they take
It comes with a price

They look you in the eye
Lie straight to your face
They believe their own lies
Now that is a disgrace

Their next hideous trait
Is that of being a cheat
They march to the music
Of their own twisted beat

If you question their lies
You are told, you are insane
They try twist their stories
As they try shift the blame

They shout the loudest
As their control slips away
For the power that they had
It no longer holds sway

When they look in the mirror
They never see what's inside
That the person looking back
Now has no place to hide

They may treat you badly
Make it all your own fault
They can never get the key
To your heart, that's your vault

*ML 2022*

---

We all have met, worked, befriended the manipulators. They are a toxic environment to be around. Get rid of them.

## Time

The most precious thing
It costs nothing it's free
It's "time" and it is
The roots of your tree

You don't own time
You cannot lock it away
It ticks by every second
Of each and every day

Time waits for no one
It never looks back
Don't try to kill time
Keep your life on track

Don't go complaining
'I don't have the time'
You alone are responsible
Until the last bell chimes

Don't waste your time
Don't look back in regret
Because all that it does
Is cause loads of upset

Time heals everything
It feeds your very soul
To even sit in silence
Can unearth your true role

Time it is the present
A present is this time
As people try to take it
Say 'I'm sorry this is mine'

*ML 2022*

---

It's our time and we decide how to use it. But you only have the present and use it well.

## Decluttering

I opened the wardrobe
I took a look at the rack
Oh how in the World
Did I buy half that tack

I looked at one shirt
You'd only wear at Halloween
When you answer the door
And want people to scream

Out with the bin bag
It's full to the neck
I'm dumping my past
I don't give a feck

Open up the drawers
The are so full of trash
Into the bin it goes
It's cleared in a flash

From there to my head
There's loads there to clear
Past patterns of your life
Being undervalued and fear

Take all that negativity
That runs around your head
And once and for all
Put that rubbish to bed

I have made up my mind
I set goals to achieve
By changing my perception
I allowed myself to believe

Wow I feel so lighter
My body it feels so new
My future is so amazing
I'm now my own guru

*ML2022*

---

We have to clear out the rubbish in our mind every so often.

## Life as a fixer

The challenge in our life
Is to try fix oneself
But as carers and givers
We put us on a shelf

As we muddle through life
Helping all in our reach
Then Spirit does whisper
Please rest I do beseech

So you worry about others
You have anguish and stress
But all that this does
Is leave your life in a mess

You can give up your love
You can give them advice
But it's only the truth
That will often suffice

So no longer will I be
The bin where you dump
The person that has to
Drag you over each bump

People will drain you
Your energy they will sap
They just don't realise
That you're not just on tap

Only you can take care
Of the person that's you
Let everybody else
Do what they need to do

*ML 2022*

---

If you try to be everyone's fixer you only drain yourself.

## Musings of life

You can add some facts
By using your imagination
But to imagine your facts
Can cause consternation

Life just like in chess
You can be cute as a fox
But the pieces you play with
Go back into the same box

If your mind is busy
And everything is just toil
That's like being a flower
Without any water or soil

You have to take stock
It's important for your growth
Learn kindness and gratitude
Make them your lifeboat

Your kindness and gratitude
With love it is a must
These things last forever
Even when the body is dust

This life of ours now
Is just rolling on by
Don't waste not a minute
For one day you will die

The kindness and gratitude
It must come from within
It will change your outlook
For you that's a win, win.

*ML2022*

---

Kindness and gratitude are keys to a happy life.

# Zoom call to God

Good morning dear God
Something just is not right
Why the hell in this World
Does everyone have to fight

Well you see it's like this
Where egos do abound
There's not enough love
In the World to go round

Just look at your island
It's beautiful and green
But the energy to power it
Is still mostly unclean

It's not the World leaders
Who decide what you need
You all have free choice
But most people choose greed

Things now are changing
The energy is moving fast
People are taking note
From the mistakes of the past

It won't be long now
The ascension is near
It's time to feel the joy
To smile with some cheer

Call in your Guardian Angel
Call in your Spirit Guide
They are here to help you
They are always by your side

*ML2022*

---

We all have free choice so use it wisely for the benefit of the World.

## Destiny woes

We all have our goals
To get to a destination
But all that does do
Is put you under obligation

You may make your destiny
To go meet your soulmate
But people like that
Aren't served on a plate

Or maybe it's your destiny
To have loads of wealth
But what really matters
Is having good health

Or maybe it's your destiny
To own your own home
But it's only a dwelling
Made of concrete and stone

Is it your destiny to have
Everyone's approval of "me"
But would anyone jump in
If you were drowning at sea

While others their destiny
Is to be wealthy and secure
But the happiest people
Are those that are poor

So if your destiny is
To get to the next place
Realise that happiness
Is living here in this place

*ML 2022*

---

We spend so much time saying I will be happy when I get here or achieve this. But true happiness is in the now and the journey.

## Things to ponder

Is it the power of love
Or is it the love of power
One of these things
Turns the sweet into sour

We all have done courses
That just push motivation
But the one you really need
Is one full of inspiration

You can think of the future
You can dwell on the past
But live in the present
For your happiness to last

If you lose a real friend
Even though they are gone
You can't lose the feeling
Of knowing you had one

Have you got the courage
To follow your own path
Even though you do know
It will incur someone's wrath

Think of your life here
And the choices you make
Even if it is a wrong one
You can correct that mistake

All of the above nuggets
Are wisdom for you to see
Each verse has a message
From the beautiful life tree

*ML 2022*

---

Sometimes we get inspiration from the strangest of places and words.

## Subjective experience

The World now around us
Hmmmm is it just me
I need to be more grounded
Like the roots of a tree

I cannot change the World
Within which I now live
Imagine your sands of life
Being run through a sieve

What's left in the sieve
Are things you don't need
The good stuff slides through
It's those feelings you feed

Go change your subjective
Of how you do think
A nice happy thought
Will just get you in sync

Anticipate the good things
Seek only the very best
The reticular activity system
It will do all the rest

So have your chin up
The powers in our hands
By subjectively changing
Your happiness will expand

The moral of the story
Nothing is set in stone
Imagine your negativity
Melting away like a cone

*ML 2022*

---

Again, nothing we feel cannot be changed or altered, we have free choice.

## The last flight

So the time has come
This is your last flight
As you plan to leave
Put this World out of sight

So what kind of luggage
Do you think you can bring
Is it all your possessions
Can you take everything

You load up the big case
To the desk you are bound
But nobody is there
Not a soul to be found

What can you do now
But change to the small case
Take your dearest possessions
That you got in this place

The rest of your life
Is left behind on the floor
All your amassed wealth
Is totally useless anymore

You head up to security
One person at the gate
They are shaking their head
Sorry no luggage, too late

Did you love many people
Did you do some good deeds
Was it kindness and gratitude
The things you did feed

You can bring your kind deeds
Your prayers and your love
That's all that has value
In the land that's above

*ML 2022*

---

When we leave our earthly bodies there isn't anything we can bring except our good deeds and love, it does not matter how rich you were. You can't buy your way into heaven, you earn it with goodness.

## The wonder of life

Did you ever wonder
What makes you smile
When did you last laugh
Was it not for a while

Did you ever wonder
What is a real friend
Do you ever consider
That a lot just pretend

Did you ever wonder
Why door's just open wide
When you're in a good place
And your going with the tide

Did you ever wonder
Why the things you know
All came from hard lessons
In order that you grow

Did you ever wonder
Why we listen to bad news
When the decision is ours
We are the ones that choose

Did you ever wonder
Why you made a decision
That you never thought out
Or visualised through a vision

Did you ever wonder
Why teachings from above
No matter what religion
Just all boil down to LOVE

*ML 2022*

---

At the end of the day it's only love that counts. We are tested in life to teach us lessons we need to learn to progress.

## The fridge analogy

What is an auld fridge
It's a place that you store
All of those nice foods
That feeds you and more

You have your own fridge
It's there you will find
All of your own thoughts
It's just called your mind

So you open your fridge
Only good food is inside
Anything that's gone off
It has no place to hide

You look at the content
If it says out of date
It serves you no purpose
The rubbish bin is it's fate

But there in our minds
There's thoughts from the past
They are there to make sure
That your happiness won't last

When you open the door
Of your fridge just think
Would you leave anything in it
That's gone off and would stink

Your mind is your fridge
The thoughts are the food
Make sure they are positive
To maintain the right mood

*ML 2022*

---

We all have a fridge, so when you open the door, stop and think about your own fridge in your head.

## My 3D day

There I was so happy
Sitting on my throne
Then I just started
To look at my iPhone

There's loads of messages
But I was just not myself
I should have realised
Put the phone on the shelf

Respond do not react
But react I did do
But today I look back
Oh how silly were you

What a waste of energy
What a waste of time
Down the hole I went
My poor brain in decline

There I was thinking
I was above the 3D
But I returned to it
This was definitely not me

But the momentum took off
I was rowing up stream
Going around in a circle
This is all a bad dream

To the bed I later went
Threw 3D in the bin
I woke up this morning
I started from within

I no longer have judgement
With compassion I smile
Everyone is just different
Life should not be a toil

*ML 2022*

---

We all have days when we revert back to 3D life. Acknowledging it for what it is and moving on is the key.

## You know it's okay

You know it's okay
To go change your mind
To protect your energy
And inner peace to find

You know it's okay
To want to be alone
To have no distractions
Especially your iPhone

You know it's okay
To just take off a day
To go relax and unwind
Go meditate and pray

You know that it's okay
To pat your own back
To know your own worth
Your accolades to stack

You know that it's okay
To laugh and giggle too
Most people are miserable
But that shouldn't be you

You know that it's okay
When something is amiss
To refrain from doing it
As it would ruin your bliss

You know that it's okay
To voice your opinion
To stand into your power
To hold your own dominion

*ML 2022*

---

The hardest thing at times is to be kind to ourselves and cut us some slack. It's okay not to be perfect, and be yourself.

# I heard kids playing

Do you just remember
The joy of being a child
When all of your thoughts
Were wonderful and wild

There were no restrictions
You walked on the moon
You owned a space ship
It was your bedroom

Boys sat playing with Lego
Their imagination in flow
Nothing would stop them
Every possibility would grow

Girls they played house
Combed the dolls hair
Dressed them flamboyantly
No one questioned their flair

There were no restrictions
There was no list of "to do"
You were never even hungry
Till your mother called you

But then we were all given
Some structure and rules
You became about as useful
As a one legged stool

Your imagination was curbed
You joined the rat race
The struggle of your life
Written all over your face

Go find that inner child
It just wants to go play
Realise that your happiness
Can return to you today

*ML 2022*

---

Remember as kids we laughed, dreamed, played. But we were shackled by society. Get rid of those shackles.

## Sail on

Think of your brain
As being like a boat
If it is totally overloaded
Sure the thing can't float

Your brain is the boat
It's all loaded with files
We gathered them up
We keep them in piles

As we sail our boat
We file more and more
Until we can't figure out
The sea from the shore

Then all of a sudden
We can see no land
Our boat it starts sinking
In our minds quicksand

So you lessen your load
Old cargo you dump
All the learned behaviour
That kept you in a slump

I choose a new mantra
Positivity will I save
So my boat will flow gently
Bringing the peace I crave

For where I point my boat
That is my destination
Don't point it up stream
That causes consternation

*ML 2023*

---

If we take on board too much rubbish in life we are going to sink into the oblivion of uselessness. Clear out your pool daily.

## Observe don't absorb

Going out to socialise
I'm protected within an inch
When I'm out in company
My bubble does not flinch

As I sit and chat to all
Some ask you for advice
On how to be intuitive
To hear the inner voice

They are trying to evolve
But 3D has its hold
I tell them to have patience
Just to let it all unfold

As I explained the process
To go and search inside
I could see the realisation
There was no place to hide

They struggled with the idea
That vibration is the key
The higher the energy is
The better life will be

I gave them our podcast
That will make you smile
How pub grub was invented
And things that are worthwhile

These things I did observe
In my bubble I was good
I did not absorb a thing
And that I understood

*ML 2022*

---

Observe what goes on around you, bubble up and don't absorb it.
Keep protecting yourself.

## The Spirit World

I live now in a place
There is no ego or hate
I knew I was home
When I walked in the gate

A tunnel of white light
Leads the way to my home
I can now make contact
Without using an iPhone

I can see a huge lake
There are flowers and trees
I can smell the sweetness
The honey from the bees

I am now just an energy
I am love, compassion, and joy
To drama and negativity
I'm so glad to say goodbye

My ancestors are all here
I'm with my mum and dad
To be smothered in love
Of that you will be glad

What was I worried about
Why was there a fear
The thoughts and anxiety
They no longer exist here

There is no pain or anguish
My body is left behind
My soul is just soaring
I have left that old grind

Do not fear your ending
It is the start of your bliss
Your time here on Earth
I promise you won't miss

*ML 2022*

---

Life after we leave this planet is so amazing. Your body is only a vessel to house your soul while you learn more lessons and evolve.

## Moral compass

What is a compass
It gives you direction
If you're on a wrong path
You can make a correction

What are your morals
What do they really mean
For so many they're a torch
When turned off, no beam

You wander in the dark
Going around and around
Living without consequences
But no happiness to be found

You jump back and forth
In search of those highs
But it's not very long
And all you have is a sigh

Then out of the blue
You are handed a choice
In your hands is a compass
It's got morals and it's nice

Suddenly you realise
There are things called "don't"
They make our life miserable
So you change them to "won't"

Your compass is now working
It's all there in your mind
If everyone would follow it
We could so change Mankind

*ML2022*

---

Having a moral compass can only bring happiness. When you sleep at night it's nice to know you done the right thing.

## Have I

Have I touched a soul
Have I spread the light
Am I a candle in darkness
Am I the moon at night

Have I given a hand
Have I lessened the pain
Am I the illness or cure
Washing powder for a stain

Have I increased the vibration
Have I brought some joy
Am I the energy needed
These things you can't buy

Have I forgiven others
Have I deleted the past
Or do I hold old grudges
Which makes the misery last

Have I looked deep inside
Have I examined the "me"
Can I live happily by myself
Or do I need the family tree

Have I listened intently
Have I given good direction
Or am I like a politician
Would say anything for election

Have I, have I, have I
You see it's not so nice
One day people will see
Their actions have a price

*ML2022*

---

Remember karma is a bitch, so make sure your karma when it comes back is all good.